AF270661

GEMINI

by Elizabeth Andrews

WELCOME TO DiscoverRoo!

This book is filled with videos, puzzles, games, and more! Scan the QR codes* while you read, or visit the website below to make this book pop.

popbooksonline.com/gemini

abdobooks.com

Published by Pop!, a division of ABDO, PO Box 398166, Minneapolis, Minnesota 55439. Copyright © 2026 by Abdo Consulting Group, Inc. International copyrights reserved in all countries. No part of this book may be reproduced in any form without written permission from the publisher. DiscoverRoo™ is a trademark and logo of Pop!.

Printed in the United States of America, North Mankato, Minnesota.
042025
082025

Cover Photo: Splendoura Prints; Shutterstock Images
Interior Photos: Getty Images; Shutterstock Images
Editor: Tyler Gieseke
Series Designer: Laura Graphenteen

Library of Congress Control Number: 2024948394

Publisher's Cataloging-in-Publication Data
Names: Andrews, Elizabeth, author.
Title: Gemini / by Elizabeth Andrews
Description: Minneapolis, Minnesota : Pop!, 2026 | Series: Zodiac signs | Includes online resources and index
Identifiers: ISBN 9781098247904 (lib. bdg.) | ISBN 9781098248444 (ebook)
Subjects: LCSH: Gemini (Astrology)--Juvenile literature. | Twins (Astrology)--Juvenile literature. | Zodiac--Juvenile literature. | Astrology--Juvenile literature. | Astrology--Charts, diagrams, etc.--Juvenile literature.
Classification: DDC 133.52--dc23

*Scanning QR codes requires a web-enabled smart device with a QR code reader app and a camera.

TABLE OF CONTENTS

CHAPTER 1
Meet the Gemini! 4

CHAPTER 2
History of Astrology 12

CHAPTER 3
The Communicator 18

CHAPTER 4
The Duality of Gemini 24

Making Connections 30
Glossary 31
Index 32
Online Resources 32

MEET THE GEMINI!

Gemini is the third sign of the zodiac. Geminis are born between May 21 and June 21. When people ask for your "star sign," they are likely asking for your sun sign. This is the zodiac sign the sun appeared to be in at your birth.

Lily of the Valley

GEMINI

constellation

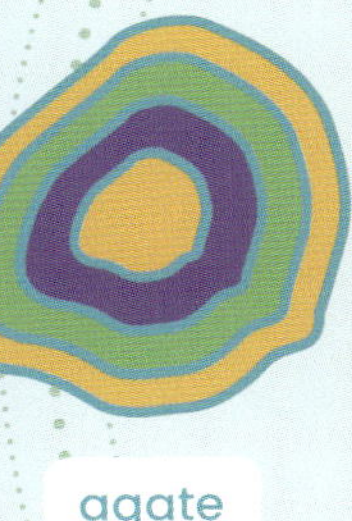

masculine

agate

mutable

5

numbers

9

WED

ZODIAC CALENDAR

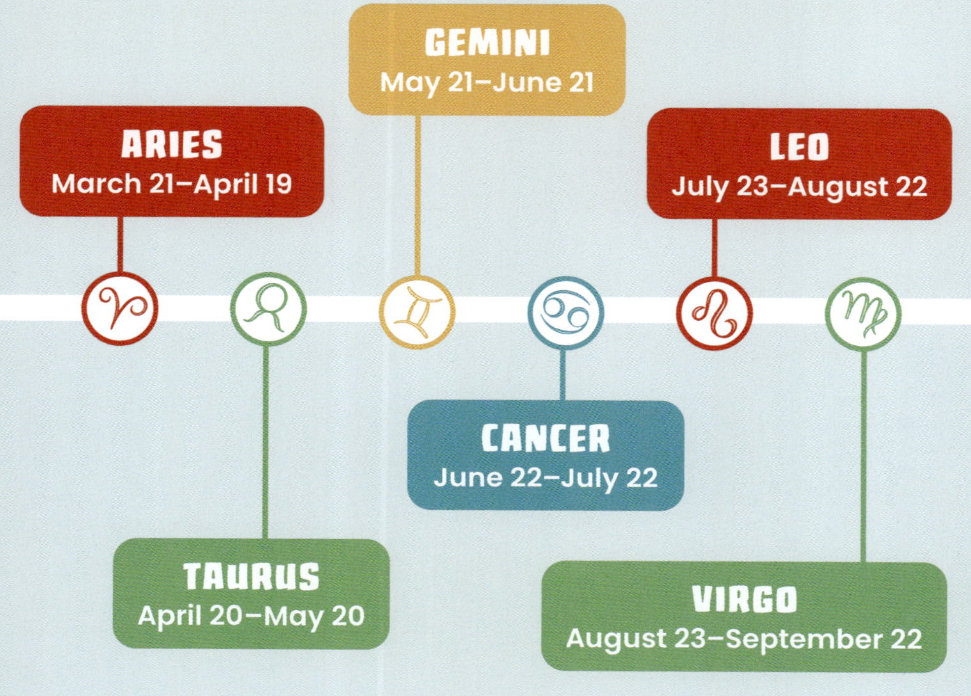

Three features help describe zodiac signs. Signs can be masculine or feminine. Each zodiac sign is given a mode. The three modes are cardinal, fixed, and mutable. Each zodiac is also

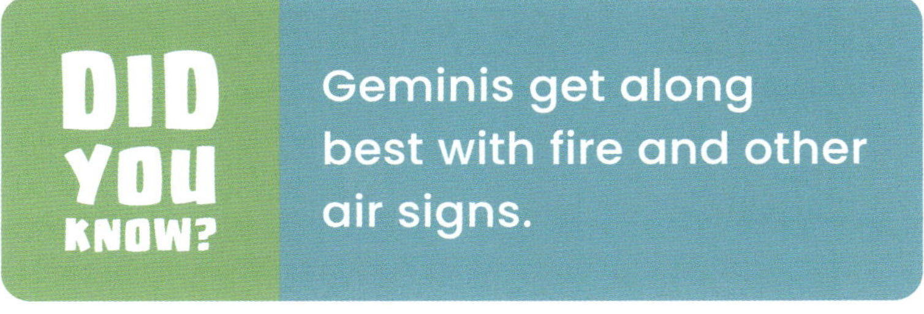

a fire, air, earth, or water sign. No zodiac

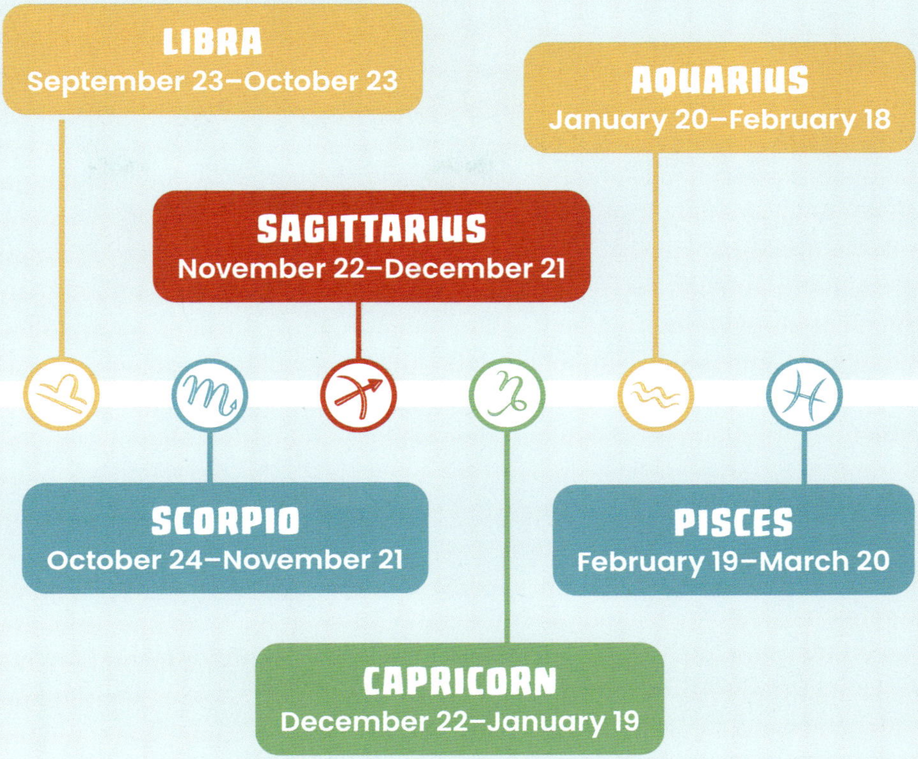

sign shares the same three features.

DID YOU KNOW? Geminis get along best with fire and other air signs.

Gemini is a masculine, mutable, air sign. People with masculine signs are reasonable and action focused. They usually say exactly what they mean. They are outgoing and strong.

Modes determine how signs interact with the outside world. Mutable signs are comfortable with change and open-minded. They are usually easygoing. Air signs are smart and talkative. They are often curious and quirky.

Mutable signs are born at the end of a season. Geminis are born at the end of spring.

Geminis are **represented** by a set
of twins. Some of the earliest astrologers
connected the Gemini **constellation** to
their twin gods of the underworld. Ancient
Greeks believed the twins were Pollux
and Castor. Pollux was the son of Zeus
and could live forever. Castor was human
and would die. Zeus put Castor and
Pollux in the stars
so they could
be together in
the heavens.

Castor and Pollux's mother was named Leda. She was a human queen.

HISTORY OF ASTROLOGY

Humans have looked for life's **spiritual** meaning since the beginning of time. They often looked to the stars for this. Astrology is the practice of reading the movements of planets and other **celestial** bodies and connecting them to life on Earth.

Some ancient people used the zodiac signs to predict future events.

Babylonians invented the zodiac in Mesopotamia over 5,000 years ago. Mesopotamia was the first known civilization. Babylon was one of the region's largest cities.

Ptolemy was an Egyptian man who studied the stars.

The zodiac is a belt of space around Earth that has 12 well-known **constellations**. Ancient people noticed that the sun seemed to move in front of these constellations throughout a year. The sun spends about a month in each constellation.

The constellations in the zodiac belt are Aries, Taurus, Gemini, Cancer, Leo, Virgo, Libra, Scorpius, Sagittarius, Capricornus, Aquarius, and Pisces. Together they make up the 12 zodiac signs. They are all **represented** by different **symbols**.

Islamic astrologers created new ways to map and measure stars.

THE ZODIAC WHEEL

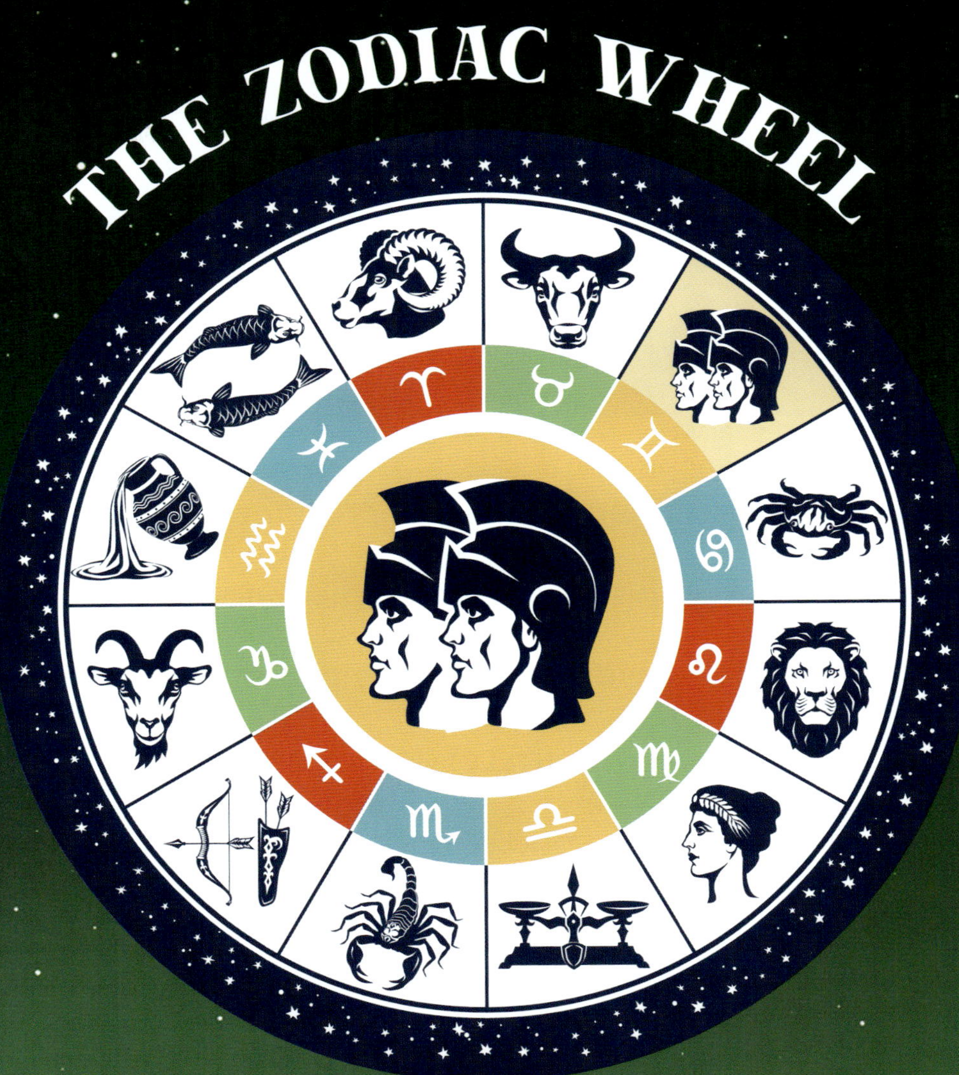

CHAPTER 3

THE COMMUNICATOR

Gemini is ruled by the planet Mercury.

Mercury is named after the quick-footed

Roman messenger god. This planet

represents all forms of communication,

such as writing and speaking. It also

rules travel. Gemini is the sign of

communication between people.

Geminis want everyone to see the world

as they do.

Geminis are a very social sign. They are playful and talkative. They can make friends easily. Geminis usually have many different groups of friends. They make connections through their wide variety of interests. Geminis love talking about the things they're interested in.

Geminis are full of curiosity. Some people say they are students of life. Geminis won't sit and let the world go by around them. Rather, they want to take part. Geminis enjoy new experiences and ask questions so they are always learning.

HUMAN CONNECTION

Gemini is thought to be the most human sign. Humans are different from animals. Their brains are bigger and stronger. They have a greater ability to understand and interact with others, and adapt to new situations. Geminis are great communicators and easily adaptable.

Geminis find the outdoors exciting. There is much to discover and explore.

Geminis are
good at making
other people
laugh.

The combination of being social and curious makes Geminis clever. They are quick to understand and learn. They can be bright and funny. Geminis pick up information and ideas from their day-to-day life and the people they are with. They are great people to talk with because they are **charming**.

CHAPTER 4

THE DUALITY OF GEMINI

Geminis are multifaceted. This means they have many different sides to them. Geminis can change their personalities to fit in with any situation. At work, they can be very thoughtful. At home, they

Agates come in many color combinations.

may be goofier and more lighthearted.

Some people believe this makes Geminis

two-faced, like twins.

A major example of **duality** in Geminis is their ability to be happy and unhappy at the same time. Geminis often feel like they aren't living at their best. Because of this, they are always looking for new ideas or projects to make them feel complete. In their search, Geminis often leave tasks unfinished.

Friends of Geminis value their wit and positive energy. Geminis lift their friends out of sadness. People also go to Geminis for advice because they can offer fresh ideas and comfort. Geminis don't get too involved in their friends' problems though. It would take away from Geminis' drive for an easy and free lifestyle.

Good friends of Geminis see the sign's positives and negatives.

DID YOU KNOW? Geminis get bored easily. They need changes of scenery and a variety of friends.

Kendrick Lamar is a Gemini. Along with being a famous rapper, he is an award-winning poet.

With their skills of communicating and making friends, Geminis are excellent salespeople. They are also good **managers** because they bring excitement to teams. Geminis often become writers and performers. They like to share their ideas and adventures.

Today, astrology can answer questions about an individual. People use astrology to understand who they are and why they might do what they do. It can also help them understand other people in their life. A zodiac sign can point out personal skills, possibilities, and **internal motivations**.

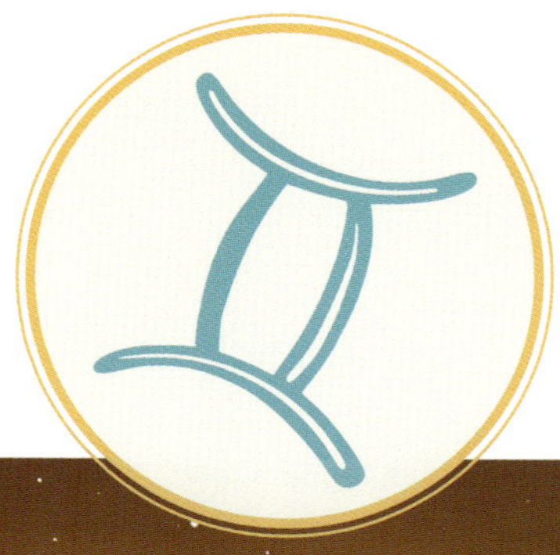

TEXT-TO-SELF

Are you a Gemini? If so, do you think the sign matches your personality? If not, what do you have in common with Geminis?

TEXT-TO-TEXT

Have you read any books about the other zodiac signs? How were those signs similar to and different from Geminis?

TEXT-TO-WORLD

With the help of an adult, look up famous Geminis. Pick one person and write a few sentences about ways that person shows Gemini qualities.

celestial — having to do with the sky or outer space.

charming — very pleasing and delightful.

constellation — a group of stars that forms a pattern.

duality — the quality of having two different or opposite parts.

internal — of, relating to, or being on the inside.

manager — the person who controls a business or acts as the leader of a plan or project.

motivation — something that makes one want to do something.

represent — to stand for or be a sign of.

spiritual — having to do with people's beliefs in things such as the soul, nature, and what happens after death.

symbol — an object or picture that represents something else.

air sign, 7–9

astrology, 12, 29

birth, 4

birth chart, 29

career, 28

challenges, 26

communication, 18–19, 21, 28

constellations, 10, 15–16

dates, 4

element, 7

Greeks, 10

masculine sign, 6, 8

Mercury, 18

Mesopotamia, 13

mode, 6, 8–9

relationships, 27

traits, 8–9, 18–21, 23–28

twins, 10, 25

zodiac belt, 15–16

DiscoverRoo! ONLINE RESOURCES

This book is filled with videos, puzzles, games, and more! Scan the QR codes* while you read, or visit the website below to make this book pop.

popbooksonline.com/gemini

*Scanning QR codes requires a web-enabled smart device with a QR code reader app and a camera.